Human Design

PROJECTORS

Workbook and Prompt Journal

A Guide To Discover Who You Really Are,
Self Love & Your Strategy and Authority as a Projector

Thanks for the invitation!

Before you start filling in your journal I suggest you print out your chart and paste (or staple) it to the inside of the front cover. It'll be a great way to refer back to your Human Design and you'll have everything at your fingertips. Happy exploring!

- Angel Jackson, 5/1 Self-Projected Projector

"It's something very important for you to understand how different you are from the majority that you live amongst."

- *Ra Uru Hu,* Founder & Messenger of the Human Design System, Speaking about Projectors

Learning about I'm a Human Design Projector has...

_____
_____
_____
_____
_____
_____
_____
_____
_____
_____
_____
_____
_____
_____
_____
_____
_____
_____
_____
_____
_____
_____
_____
_____
_____
_____
_____
_____
_____
_____
_____

Human Design Projector Strategy

<u>*Recognition and Waiting for the Invitation looks/feels like...*</u>

_____

_____

_____

_____

_____

_____

_____

_____

_____

_____

_____

_____

_____

_____

_____

_____

_____

_____

_____

_____

_____

_____

_____

_____

_____

_____

_____

Human Design Projector Strategy

How I've been recognized in the past...

_____

_____

_____

_____

_____

_____

_____

_____

_____

_____

_____

_____

_____

_____

_____

_____

_____

_____

_____

_____

_____

_____

_____

_____

_____

_____

Human Design Projector Strategy

What invitations look/feel like...

Invitations I'd like to receive...

Invitations I'd like to receive...

Invitations I'd like to receive...

Human Design Projector Not-Self Theme

Bitterness looks/feels like...

_____

_____

_____

_____

_____

_____

_____

_____

_____

_____

_____

_____

_____

_____

_____

_____

_____

_____

_____

_____

_____

_____

_____

_____

_____

_____

_____

_____

_____

_____

_____

_____

Human Design Projector Not-Self Theme

Bitterness looks/feels like...

_____
_____
_____
_____
_____
_____
_____
_____
_____
_____
_____
_____
_____
_____
_____
_____
_____
_____
_____
_____
_____
_____
_____
_____
_____
_____
_____
_____
_____
_____
_____

Human Design Projector Not-Self Theme

What can I do to avoid my Not-Self...

_____

_____

_____

_____

_____

_____

_____

_____

_____

_____

_____

_____

_____

_____

_____

_____

_____

_____

_____

_____

_____

_____

_____

_____

_____

_____

_____

Human Design Projector Signature

Success looks/feels like...

Human Design Projector Signature

Success looks/feels like...

_____
_____
_____
_____
_____
_____
_____
_____
_____
_____
_____
_____
_____
_____
_____
_____
_____
_____
_____
_____
_____
_____
_____
_____
_____
_____
_____
_____
_____
_____
_____
_____
_____

Human Design Projector Signature

Times when I felt Success...

Ways I Feel Conditioned

_____

_____

_____

_____

_____

_____

_____

_____

_____

_____

_____

_____

_____

_____

_____

_____

_____

_____

_____

_____

_____

_____

_____

_____

_____

_____

_____

_____

_____

_____

Ways I Feel Conditioned

_____
_____
_____
_____
_____
_____
_____
_____
_____
_____
_____
_____
_____
_____
_____
_____
_____
_____
_____
_____
_____
_____
_____
_____
_____
_____
_____
_____
_____
_____

Ways I Feel Conditioned

_____
_____
_____
_____
_____
_____
_____
_____
_____
_____
_____
_____
_____
_____
_____
_____
_____
_____
_____
_____
_____
_____
_____
_____
_____
_____
_____
_____
_____
_____
_____
_____

Ways I Feel Conditioned

Ways I Feel Conditioned

_____

_____

_____

_____

_____

_____

_____

_____

_____

_____

_____

_____

_____

_____

_____

_____

_____

_____

_____

_____

_____

_____

_____

_____

_____

_____

_____

_____

_____

_____

De-conditioning

I can De-condition myself by...

_____

_____

_____

_____

_____

_____

_____

_____

_____

_____

_____

_____

_____

_____

_____

_____

_____

_____

_____

_____

_____

_____

_____

_____

_____

_____

_____

_____

_____

_____

_____

_____

De-conditioning

De-conditioning

De-conditioning

My Energy As A Projector

Ways I gather energy...

_____
_____
_____
_____
_____
_____
_____
_____
_____
_____
_____
_____
_____
_____
_____
_____
_____
_____
_____
_____
_____
_____
_____
_____
_____
_____
_____
_____
_____

My Energy As A Projector

Ways I gather energy...

_____

_____

_____

_____

_____

_____

_____

_____

_____

_____

_____

_____

_____

_____

_____

_____

_____

_____

_____

_____

_____

_____

_____

_____

_____

_____

_____

_____

My Projector Authority

I'm a _____ Projector _____

That means... _____

_____

_____

_____

_____

_____

_____

_____

_____

_____

_____

_____

_____

_____

_____

_____

_____

_____

_____

_____

_____

_____

_____

_____

_____

_____

_____

_____

_____

_____

My Projector Authority

My Projector Authority

My Projector Authority

My Intuition

My Intuition

_____
_____
_____
_____
_____
_____
_____
_____
_____
_____
_____
_____
_____
_____
_____
_____
_____
_____
_____
_____
_____
_____
_____
_____
_____
_____
_____
_____
_____

Guiding As A Projector

Ways I guide others...

_____

_____

_____

_____

_____

_____

_____

_____

_____

_____

_____

_____

_____

_____

_____

_____

_____

_____

_____

_____

_____

_____

_____

_____

_____

_____

_____

_____

Guiding As A Projector

Ways I guide others...

_____
_____
_____
_____
_____
_____
_____
_____
_____
_____
_____
_____
_____
_____
_____
_____
_____
_____
_____
_____
_____
_____
_____
_____
_____
_____
_____
_____
_____

Guiding As A Projector

Ways I guide others...

_____

_____

_____

_____

_____

_____

_____

_____

_____

_____

_____

_____

_____

_____

_____

_____

_____

_____

_____

_____

_____

_____

_____

_____

_____

_____

_____

_____

_____

_____

My Projector Profile

I'm a _____ / _____

My first line is _____ and that means... _____

_____

_____

_____

_____

_____

_____

_____

_____

_____

_____

_____

_____

_____

_____

_____

_____

_____

_____

_____

_____

_____

_____

_____

_____

_____

_____

_____

_____

_____

_____

My Human Design Profile

That also means that...
_____
_____
_____
_____
_____
_____
_____
_____
_____
_____
_____
_____
_____
_____
_____
_____
_____
_____
_____
_____
_____
_____
_____
_____
_____
_____
_____
_____
_____
_____
_____
_____

My Human Design Profile

What I've learned so far on this journey is that my first line...

_____

_____

_____

_____

_____

_____

_____

_____

_____

_____

_____

_____

_____

_____

_____

_____

_____

_____

_____

_____

_____

_____

_____

_____

_____

_____

_____

_____

_____

_____

_____

_____

_____

My Human Design Profile

Cont'd...

My Human Design Profile

My second line is _____ and that means... _____

_____
_____
_____
_____
_____
_____
_____
_____
_____
_____
_____
_____
_____
_____
_____
_____
_____
_____
_____
_____
_____
_____
_____
_____
_____
_____
_____
_____
_____
_____

My Human Design Profile

That also means...
_____

_____
_____
_____
_____
_____
_____
_____
_____
_____
_____
_____
_____
_____
_____
_____
_____
_____
_____
_____
_____
_____
_____
_____
_____
_____
_____
_____
_____
_____
_____

My Human Design Profile

What I've learned so far on this journey is that my second line...

_____

_____

_____

_____

_____

_____

_____

_____

_____

_____

_____

_____

_____

_____

_____

_____

_____

_____

_____

_____

_____

_____

_____

_____

_____

My Human Design Profile

More notes about my Profile...

My Human Design Profile

<u>Even more notes about my Profile because I'm a Projector...</u>

_____

_____

_____

_____

_____

_____

_____

_____

_____

_____

_____

_____

_____

_____

_____

_____

_____

_____

_____

_____

_____

_____

_____

_____

_____

_____

_____

_____

_____

_____

My Human Design Profile

More notes about my Profile, how I see myself and how others see me...

My Human Design Profile

More notes about my Profile, how I see myself and how others see me...

_____

_____

_____

_____

_____

_____

_____

_____

_____

_____

_____

_____

_____

_____

_____

_____

_____

_____

_____

_____

_____

_____

_____

_____

_____

_____

_____

_____

My Definition

I have a _____ Definition.

That means... _____

_____

_____

_____

_____

_____

_____

_____

_____

_____

_____

_____

_____

_____

_____

_____

_____

_____

_____

_____

_____

_____

_____

_____

_____

_____

_____

_____

_____

_____

My Definition

That also means that...

My Incarnation Cross

My Incarnation Cross is...

_____

_____

_____

_____

_____

_____

_____

_____

_____

_____

_____

_____

_____

_____

_____

_____

_____

_____

_____

_____

_____

_____

_____

_____

_____

_____

_____

_____

_____

_____

_____

_____

_____

My Incarnation Cross

My Incarnation Cross also tells me that...

_____

_____

_____

_____

_____

_____

_____

_____

_____

_____

_____

_____

_____

_____

_____

_____

_____

_____

_____

_____

_____

_____

_____

_____

_____

_____

_____

_____

_____

_____

_____

_____

_____

My Incarnation Cross

My Incarnation Cross Gates are...

My Incarnation Cross

<u>My Incarnation Cross Gates are...</u>

_____

_____

_____

_____

_____

_____

_____

_____

_____

_____

_____

_____

_____

_____

_____

_____

_____

_____

_____

_____

_____

_____

_____

_____

_____

_____

_____

_____

_____

My Incarnation Cross

My Incarnation Cross Channels are...

My Incarnation Cross

My Incarnation Cross Channels are...

My Defined Centers

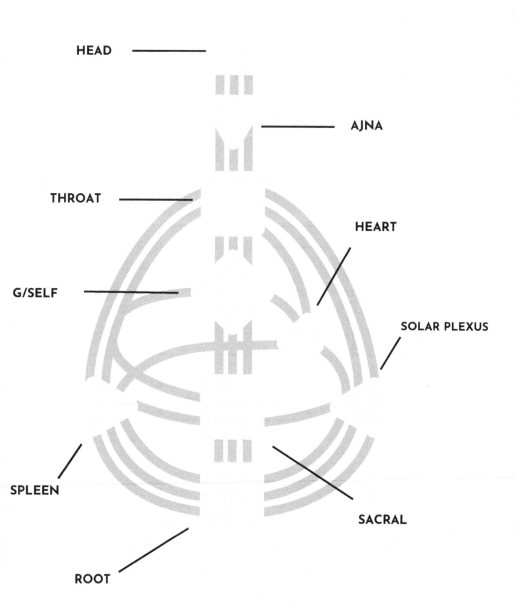

HEAD

AJNA

THROAT

HEART

G/SELF

SOLAR PLEXUS

SPLEEN

SACRAL

ROOT

My Defined Centers

My Defined Center(s)...

_____

_____

_____

_____

_____

_____

_____

_____

_____

_____

_____

_____

_____

_____

_____

_____

_____

_____

_____

_____

_____

_____

_____

_____

_____

_____

_____

_____

_____

_____

_____

_____

My Defined Centers

My Defined Center(s)...

My Defined Centers

My Defined Center(s)...

My Defined Centers

My Defined Center(s)...

My Defined Centers

My Defined Center(s)...

_____
_____
_____
_____
_____
_____
_____
_____
_____
_____
_____
_____
_____
_____
_____
_____
_____
_____
_____
_____
_____
_____
_____
_____
_____
_____
_____
_____
_____

My Defined Centers

My Defined Center(s)...

My Defined Centers

My Defined Center(s)...

_____

_____

_____

_____

_____

_____

_____

_____

_____

_____

_____

_____

_____

_____

_____

_____

_____

_____

_____

_____

_____

_____

_____

_____

_____

_____

_____

_____

_____

_____

_____

_____

My Defined Centers

My Defined Center(s)...

My Undefined Centers

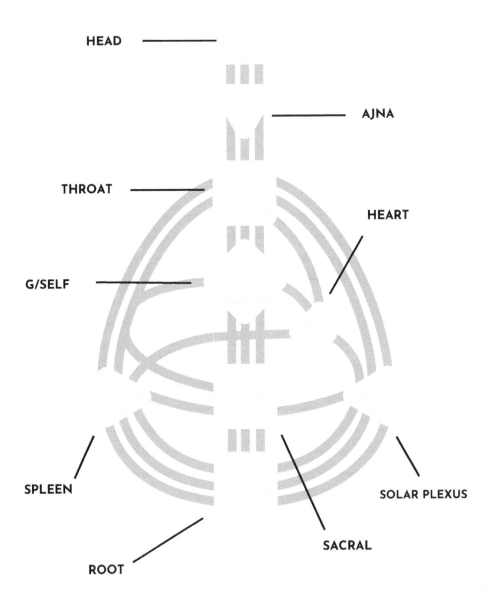

HEAD

AJNA

THROAT

HEART

G/SELF

SPLEEN

SOLAR PLEXUS

SACRAL

ROOT

My Undefined Centers

My Undefined Center(s)...

_____

_____

_____

_____

_____

_____

_____

_____

_____

_____

_____

_____

_____

_____

_____

_____

_____

_____

_____

_____

_____

_____

_____

_____

_____

_____

_____

_____

_____

_____

_____

_____

_____

My Undefined Centers

<u>My Undefined Center(s)...</u>

_____

_____

_____

_____

_____

_____

_____

_____

_____

_____

_____

_____

_____

_____

_____

_____

_____

_____

_____

_____

_____

_____

_____

_____

_____

_____

_____

_____

_____

_____

_____

_____

_____

_____

_____

_____

My Undefined Centers

My Undefined Center(s)...

My Undefined Centers

My Undefined Center(s)...

My Undefined Centers

My Undefined Center(s)...

My Undefined Centers

My Undefined Center(s)...

My Undefined Centers

My Undefined Center(s)...

_____
_____
_____
_____
_____
_____
_____
_____
_____
_____
_____
_____
_____
_____
_____
_____
_____
_____
_____
_____
_____
_____
_____
_____
_____
_____
_____
_____
_____
_____
_____
_____
_____
_____
_____
_____
_____

My Undefined Centers

My Undefined Center(s)...

_____
_____
_____
_____
_____
_____
_____
_____
_____
_____
_____
_____
_____
_____
_____
_____
_____
_____
_____
_____
_____
_____
_____
_____
_____
_____
_____
_____
_____
_____

My Activated Gates

_____
_____
_____
_____
_____
_____
_____
_____
_____
_____
_____
_____
_____
_____
_____
_____
_____
_____
_____
_____
_____
_____
_____
_____
_____
_____
_____
_____
_____

My Activated Gates

_____
_____
_____
_____
_____
_____
_____
_____
_____
_____
_____
_____
_____
_____
_____
_____
_____
_____
_____
_____
_____
_____
_____
_____
_____
_____
_____
_____
_____
_____

My Activated Gates

My Activated Gates

_____
_____
_____
_____
_____
_____
_____
_____
_____
_____
_____
_____
_____
_____
_____
_____
_____
_____
_____
_____
_____
_____
_____
_____
_____
_____
_____
_____
_____

My Activated Gates

My Activated Gates

_____
_____
_____
_____
_____
_____
_____
_____
_____
_____
_____
_____
_____
_____
_____
_____
_____
_____
_____
_____
_____
_____
_____
_____
_____
_____
_____
_____
_____
_____
_____

My Activated Gates

My Activated Gates

_____

_____

_____

_____

_____

_____

_____

_____

_____

_____

_____

_____

_____

_____

_____

_____

_____

_____

_____

_____

_____

_____

_____

_____

_____

_____

_____

_____

_____

My Activated Gates

My Activated Gates

_____

_____

_____

_____

_____

_____

_____

_____

_____

_____

_____

_____

_____

_____

_____

_____

_____

_____

_____

_____

_____

_____

_____

_____

_____

_____

_____

_____

_____

_____

My Activated Gates

My Activated Gates

_____
_____
_____
_____
_____
_____
_____
_____
_____
_____
_____
_____
_____
_____
_____
_____
_____
_____
_____
_____
_____
_____
_____
_____
_____
_____
_____
_____
_____
_____
_____
_____

My Activated Gates

My Hanging Gates

My Hanging Gates

My Hanging Gates

My Hanging Gates

My Hanging Gates

My Hanging Gates

My Hanging Gates

My Hanging Gates

My Hanging Gates

My Hanging Gates

My Hanging Gates

_____
_____
_____
_____
_____
_____
_____
_____
_____
_____
_____
_____
_____
_____
_____
_____
_____
_____
_____
_____
_____
_____
_____
_____
_____
_____
_____
_____
_____

My Hanging Gates

My Hanging Gates

_____
_____
_____
_____
_____
_____
_____
_____
_____
_____
_____
_____
_____
_____
_____
_____
_____
_____
_____
_____
_____
_____
_____
_____
_____
_____
_____
_____
_____
_____
_____

My Human Design Channels

My Human Design Channels

My Human Design Channels

My Human Design Channels

My Human Design Channels

My Human Design Channels

My Human Design Channels

_____
_____
_____
_____
_____
_____
_____
_____
_____
_____
_____
_____
_____
_____
_____
_____
_____
_____
_____
_____
_____
_____
_____
_____
_____
_____
_____
_____
_____
_____
_____
_____

My Human Design Channels

My Human Design Variable (Transformations)

Digestion
_____

My Human Design Variable (Transformations)

Digestion _____

_____
_____
_____
_____
_____
_____
_____
_____
_____
_____
_____
_____
_____
_____
_____
_____
_____
_____
_____
_____
_____
_____
_____
_____
_____
_____
_____
_____
_____

My Human Design Variable (Transformations)

Digestion

_____

My Human Design Variable (Transformations)

Environment

My Human Design Variable (Transformations)

Environment

_____

_____

_____

_____

_____

_____

_____

_____

_____

_____

_____

_____

_____

_____

_____

_____

_____

_____

_____

_____

_____

_____

_____

_____

_____

_____

_____

_____

_____

_____

_____

_____

_____

_____

My Human Design Variable (Transformations)

Environment

My Human Design Variable (Transformations)

Perspective

My Human Design Variable (Transformations)

Perspective _____

_____

_____

_____

_____

_____

_____

_____

_____

_____

_____

_____

_____

_____

_____

_____

_____

_____

_____

_____

_____

_____

_____

_____

_____

_____

_____

_____

_____

_____

_____

_____

_____

My Human Design Variable (Transformations)

Perspective

My Human Design Variable (Transformations)

Awareness

My Human Design Variable (Transformations)

Awareness

My Human Design Variable (Transformations)

Awareness _____

_____

_____

_____

_____

_____

_____

_____

_____

_____

_____

_____

_____

_____

_____

_____

_____

_____

_____

_____

_____

_____

_____

_____

_____

_____

_____

_____

_____

_____

My Planets & Gates

My Conscious Planets, Personality, (Black column) is:
What I realize about myself, what I'm aware of about myself.

Insert Gate # ➝

The SUN in Human Design represents...

My Conscious Sun is in Gate _____ , the Gate of

My Planets & Gates

My Conscious Planets, Personality, (Black column) is:

What I realize about myself, what I'm aware of about myself.

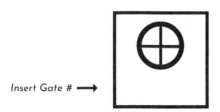

Insert Gate # ➝

The EARTH in Human Design represents...

My Conscious Earth is in Gate _____, the Gate of

My Planets & Gates

My Conscious Planets, Personality, (Black column) is: _____

What I realize about myself, what I'm aware of about myself. _____

Insert Gate # ➡

The MOON in Human Design represents... _____

_____

_____

My Conscious Moon is in Gate _____, the Gate of _____

_____

_____

_____

_____

_____

_____

_____

_____

_____

_____

_____

_____

_____

_____

_____

My Planets & Gates

My Conscious Planets, Personality, (Black column) is: _____

What I realize about myself, what I'm aware of about myself. _____

Insert Gate # ➡

The **NORTH NODE** in Human Design represents... _____

_____

_____

My Conscious North Node is in Gate _____ , the Gate of _____

_____

_____

_____

_____

_____

_____

_____

_____

_____

_____

_____

_____

My Planets & Gates

My Conscious Planets, Personality, (Black column) is: _____
What I realize about myself, what I'm aware of about myself. _____

Insert Gate # ➡

The **SOUTH NODE** in Human Design represents... _____

_____
_____

My Conscious South Node is in Gate _____ , the Gate of _____

_____
_____
_____
_____
_____
_____
_____
_____
_____
_____
_____
_____
_____
_____
_____

My Planets & Gates

My Conscious Planets, Personality, (Black column) is:

What I realize about myself, what I'm aware of about myself.

Insert Gate # ⟶

Mercury in Human Design represents...

My Conscious Mercury is in Gate _____ , the Gate of _____

My Planets & Gates

My Conscious Planets, Personality, (Black column) is:
What I realize about myself, what I'm aware of about myself.

Insert Gate # ➞

VENUS in Human Design represents...

My Conscious Venus is in Gate _____ , the Gate of

My Planets & Gates

My Conscious Planets, Personality, (Black column) is:

What I realize about myself, what I'm aware of about myself.

Insert Gate # ➡️ [♂ symbol in box]

MARS in Human Design represents...

My Conscious Mars is in Gate _____ , the Gate of _____

My Planets & Gates

My Conscious Planets, Personality, (Black column) is:

What I realize about myself, what I'm aware of about myself.

Insert Gate # ➡

$$4$$

JUPITER in Human Design represents...

My Conscious Jupiter is in Gate _____, the Gate of _____

My Planets & Gates

My Conscious Planets, Personality, (Black column) is:

What I realize about myself, what I'm aware of about myself.

Insert Gate # ⟶

SATURN in Human Design represents...

My Conscious Saturn is in Gate _____ , the Gate of

My Planets & Gates

My Conscious Planets, Personality, (Black column) is: _____

What I realize about myself, what I'm aware of about myself. _____

Insert Gate # ➡

URANUS in Human Design represents... _____

_____

_____

My Conscious Uranus is in Gate _____ , the Gate of _____

_____

_____

_____

_____

_____

_____

_____

_____

_____

_____

_____

_____

_____

_____

_____

My Planets & Gates

My Conscious Planets, Personality, (Black column) is:
What I realize about myself, what I'm aware of about myself.

Insert Gate # ➡️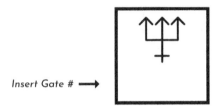

NEPTUNE in Human Design represents...

My Conscious Neptune is in Gate _____, the Gate of _____

My Planets & Gates

My Conscious Planets, Personality, (Black column) is: ______

What I realize about myself, what I'm aware of about myself. ______

Insert Gate # →

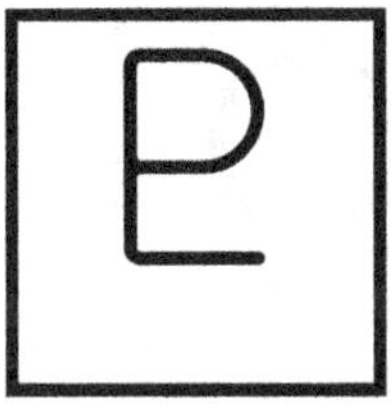

PLUTO in Human Design represents... ______

______

______

My Conscious Pluto is in Gate ______, the Gate of ______

______

______

______

______

______

______

______

______

______

______

______

______

______

______

______

My Planets & Gates

My Unconscious Planets (Red column) is:_____
_What I realize about myself, what I'm aware of about myself._____

Insert Gate # ➡

The SUN in Human Design represents..._____
_____
_____

My Unconscious Sun is in Gate_____, the Gate of_____
_____
_____
_____
_____
_____
_____
_____
_____
_____
_____
_____
_____
_____

My Planets & Gates

My Unconscious Planets (Red column) is:
What I realize about myself, what I'm aware of about myself.

Insert Gate # ➡

The EARTH in Human Design represents...

_____

_____

My Unconscious Earth is in Gate _____ , the Gate of _____

_____

_____

_____

_____

_____

_____

_____

_____

_____

_____

_____

_____

_____

_____

My Planets & Gates

My Unconscious Planets (Red column) is: _____

What I realize about myself, what I'm aware of about myself. _____

Insert Gate # ➡️

The MOON in Human Design represents... _____

_____

_____

My Unconscious Moon is in Gate _____, the Gate of _____

_____

_____

_____

_____

_____

_____

_____

_____

_____

_____

_____

_____

_____

_____

My Planets & Gates

My Unconscious Planets (Red column) is: _____
What I realize about myself, what I'm aware of about myself. _____

Insert Gate # ➝

The NORTH NODE in Human Design represents... _____

_____

_____

My Unconscious North Node is in Gate _____ , the Gate of _____

_____

_____

_____

_____

_____

_____

_____

_____

_____

_____

_____

_____

_____

_____

_____

My Planets & Gates

My Unconscious Planets (Red column) is:

What I realize about myself, what I'm aware of about myself.

Insert Gate # ➡

The SOUTH NODE in Human Design represents...

My Unconscious South Node is in Gate _____ , the Gate of _____

My Planets & Gates

My Unconscious Planets (Red column) is: _____
What I realize about myself, what I'm aware of about myself. _____

Insert Gate # ⟶ ☿

Mercury in Human Design represents... _____

_____

_____

My Unconscious Mercury is in Gate _____ , the Gate of _____

_____

_____

_____

_____

_____

_____

_____

_____

_____

_____

_____

_____

_____

_____

My Planets & Gates

My Unconscious Planets (Red column) is: _____

What I realize about myself, what I'm aware of about myself. _____

Insert Gate # ➡️

VENUS in Human Design represents... _____

_____

_____

My Unconscious Venus is in Gate _____ , the Gate of _____

_____

_____

_____

_____

_____

_____

_____

_____

_____

_____

_____

_____

_____

My Planets & Gates

My Unconscious Planets (Red column) is: _____

What I realize about myself, what I'm aware of about myself. _____

Insert Gate # ⟶

MARS in Human Design represents... _____

_____

_____

My Unconscious Mars is in Gate _____ , the Gate of _____

_____

_____

_____

_____

_____

_____

_____

_____

_____

_____

_____

_____

_____

My Planets & Gates

My Unconscious Planets (Red column) is:

What I realize about myself, what I'm aware of about myself.

Insert Gate # ➡️

24

JUPITER in Human Design represents...

My Unconscious Jupiter is in Gate _____, the Gate of _____

My Planets & Gates

My Unconscious Planets (Red column) is: _____

What I realize about myself, what I'm aware of about myself. _____

Insert Gate # ➡️

SATURN in Human Design represents... _____

_____

_____

My Unconscious Saturn is in Gate _____ , the Gate of _____

_____

_____

_____

_____

_____

_____

_____

_____

_____

_____

_____

_____

_____

_____

_____

My Planets & Gates

My Unconscious Planets (Red column) is: _____

What I realize about myself, what I'm aware of about myself. _____

Insert Gate # ➝

URANUS in Human Design represents... _____

_____

_____

My Unconscious Uranus is in Gate _____ , the Gate of _____

_____

_____

_____

_____

_____

_____

_____

_____

_____

_____

_____

_____

_____

My Planets & Gates

My Unconscious Planets (Red column) is:

What I realize about myself, what I'm aware of about myself.

Insert Gate # ➡

NEPTUNE in Human Design represents...

My Unconscious Neptune is in Gate _____, the Gate of _____

My Planets & Gates

My Unconscious Planets (Red column) is:

What I realize about myself, what I'm aware of about myself.

Insert Gate # ➝

PLUTO in Human Design represents...

_____

_____

_____

My Unconscious Pluto is in Gate _____, the Gate of _____

_____

_____

_____

_____

_____

_____

_____

_____

_____

_____

_____

_____

_____

Notes

_____

_____

_____

_____

_____

_____

_____

_____

_____

_____

_____

_____

_____

_____

_____

_____

_____

_____

_____

_____

_____

_____

_____

_____

_____

_____

_____

_____

_____

_____

_____

Notes

Notes

Notes

Notes

Notes

_____
_____
_____
_____
_____
_____
_____
_____
_____
_____
_____
_____
_____
_____
_____
_____
_____
_____
_____
_____
_____
_____
_____
_____
_____
_____
_____
_____
_____

Notes

_____

_____

_____

_____

_____

_____

_____

_____

_____

_____

_____

_____

_____

_____

_____

_____

_____

_____

_____

_____

_____

_____

_____

_____

_____

_____

_____

_____

_____

_____

_____

Notes

Notes

_____
_____
_____
_____
_____
_____
_____
_____
_____
_____
_____
_____
_____
_____
_____
_____
_____
_____
_____
_____
_____
_____
_____
_____
_____
_____
_____
_____
_____
_____
_____

Notes

Notes

Notes

Notes

Notes

_____
_____
_____
_____
_____
_____
_____
_____
_____
_____
_____
_____
_____
_____
_____
_____
_____
_____
_____
_____
_____
_____
_____
_____
_____
_____
_____
_____
_____
_____
_____

Notes

Notes

_____
_____
_____
_____
_____
_____
_____
_____
_____
_____
_____
_____
_____
_____
_____
_____
_____
_____
_____
_____
_____
_____
_____
_____
_____
_____
_____

Notes

Notes

Notes

Notes

Notes

Notes

Notes

Notes

Notes

Notes

Notes

Notes

Notes

Notes

Notes

Notes

Notes

_____

_____

_____

_____

_____

_____

_____

_____

_____

_____

_____

_____

_____

_____

_____

_____

_____

_____

_____

_____

_____

_____

_____

_____

_____

_____

_____

_____

_____

_____

_____

_____

_____

_____

Notes

Notes

Notes

Notes

_____
_____
_____
_____
_____
_____
_____
_____
_____
_____
_____
_____
_____
_____
_____
_____
_____
_____
_____
_____
_____
_____
_____
_____
_____
_____
_____
_____
_____
_____
_____
_____

Notes

Notes

_____
_____
_____
_____
_____
_____
_____
_____
_____
_____
_____
_____
_____
_____
_____
_____
_____
_____
_____
_____
_____
_____
_____
_____
_____
_____
_____
_____
_____
_____
_____

Notes

_____
_____
_____
_____
_____
_____
_____
_____
_____
_____
_____
_____
_____
_____
_____
_____
_____
_____
_____
_____
_____
_____
_____
_____
_____
_____
_____
_____
_____
_____
_____

Notes

Notes

Notes

_____
_____
_____
_____
_____
_____
_____
_____
_____
_____
_____
_____
_____
_____
_____
_____
_____
_____
_____
_____
_____
_____
_____
_____
_____
_____
_____
_____
_____

Notes

Notes

Notes

_____

_____

_____

_____

_____

_____

_____

_____

_____

_____

_____

_____

_____

_____

_____

_____

_____

_____

_____

_____

_____

_____

_____

_____

_____

_____

_____

_____

_____

Notes

Notes

Notes

Notes

Notes

Notes

Notes

Notes

_____

_____

_____

_____

_____

_____

_____

_____

_____

_____

_____

_____

_____

_____

_____

_____

_____

_____

_____

_____

_____

_____

_____

_____

_____

_____

_____

_____

_____

_____

_____

_____

Made in the USA
Las Vegas, NV
09 December 2023

82366141R10115